ANTHROPOS

Front cover artwork : 'Arthurian Tree'.

Copyright Anna Clarke, reproduced
with her permission and that of the editor of
Pendragon, U.K. in which it first appeared.

Frontispiece : Eric Ratcliffe in robes of the Druid Order

(i)

ANTHROPOS

ℰ

Eric Ratcliffe

WITH A SURVEY AND BIBLIOGRAPHY

OF HIS WORK BY

BRIAN LOUIS PEARCE

UNIVERSITY OF SALZBURG PRESS

1995

ANTHROPOS

First published in 1995 by the University of Salzburg Press in its series:

Salzburg Studies in English Literature :
Poetic Drama and Poetic Theory 120

Editor: JAMES HOGG

A CIP record for this book
is available from the British Library

ISBN 3-7052-0429-7

Institut für Anglistik und Amerikanistic
Akademiestrasse 24
Universität Salzburg 4/10/95
A-5020 Salzburg, Austria

CONTENTS

Part 1 (pp. A-1 to A-84)

ANTHROPOS

THE FLIP SIDE (A-75)

TURNING
STANDING ON A POINT
DIAL A DANCE, TWENTY-SIXTH CENTURY
NEAR DEATH EXPERIENCE OF ALFRED IN THE KITCHEN
THE TRANSFORMATION OF THE LESBIAN RHOMBUS
HORSE TREK
FLIES TAKE NO UMBRAGE

Part 2 (pp. B-1 to B-28)

SURVEY AND BIBLIOGRAPHY
by BRIAN LOUIS PEARCE

A SURVEY OF THE WORK OF ERIC RATCLIFFE (B-3)

BIBLIOGRAPHY (B-25)

Part 1

Anthropos

ACKNOWLEDGEMENTS

Some of these poems were published in *Abraxas, Acumen, Ammonite, Chapman, Envoi, Moonstone, Orbis, Ore, Pennine Platform, Rustic Rub, Spokes, The Poet,* and *Weyfarers.*

The poems 'Ages Unto Ages', 'Ashram', 'Century House', 'Corpse', 'Death Was No Empty Hat', 'Flies Take no Umbrage', 'Old Fragrance', 'The Maiden of the Moon's Boat', and 'The White River' appeared in previous collections, otherwise the bulk of the poetry post-dates the contents of *Fire in the Bush* (Salzburg, 1993).

AUTHOR'S NOTE

Anthropos (from the Greek = Man) is a useful generic title to cover the wordly, primitive and transcendental features of our species to which some of my poems refer. ('The Experiment' in *Fire in the Bush* attempted to see us as experimental life units of the Creator.)

Anthropos includes my own selection of poems, and is not that of Mr.Pearce, who writes on my work as a whole in Part 2 of this book.

E.R.

The Historical Flesh

SMALL SARAH

I

Deep in clays of centuries
the sunken wells of men
whose might in minor depth
disturbed and left their traces.
God counted units, these, rebirthed,
whose tongues bled words
in their own day's extension,
then, ash-moated, piled
bones above the last
red seam.

Time's ice roots knew
a thousand Abrahams,
as saltweed corpses
or, laid long by ritual,
with lapis beads and amulets
of fish, gazelle and bull.

Uncounted windlasses of will
wound down to limits
buckets of butchery or faith,
while, flesh-gated to the stars,
death pits over death pits,
confirmed their earth in-birthing
rituals of imperfection.

Villages of ice-pressed bodies
or many wintered cells
interred in silt on silt
of wandering estuaries,
in graveyard layers,
gave up few secrets.

Where shredded flags of empires
flew the hours, here pauses bone,
the faded sinews know no whipping masters;
the fallen, bronzed in suns of love,
lie with makers of disaster.
As willows green the lightpath ghosts
and beaded phantom cardinals
count off the passing pyres,
their atoms and the wolverines'
rest equally in stone.

II

In the fire-ape tree, master,
i saw her, i will rejoice her
with mouth song, pull her down
to our travelling ground.
Let her raise feet to light,
join with the sun-legged
drinking at water end,
rustle the plants for joy;

master i will show her
leaves for body cover,
two-foot firemaking,
a wood spear for sleeping
those who come too close,
a night dance for swaying
when the great fire is lighted;

master i will bring her down
for you, throw smoke boughs
at her tree. Foot leader,
her wide red swellings
will feed the small ones;

master she has seen me
looking, turned the air
in her branch home;
she will come down,
she will bend for you
if there is food about.

Let it be, master,
when the big bird flies
in the first sun,
I will fetch her;
master let it be so.

III

Small red sarah, escaping shank fur
convulsed in tree leaping,
otter hanging to your bank of leaves,
then fallen to the ground.
In your new walking
you, mother in the end cave,
warm-walled from scudding sand winds
of the plains, maker of faces of hunters,
working at dry-stick cooking, daughter carrier of bounty;
race pillar, rain shielder of small ones,
protector from the rodded lightning,
soother of the ills of venture fields,
breeder of over-beasts with their cries,
flamelit scribers of the calling walls
merged with the deep thinking darkness.
All from you, small sarah.

You were the shaped window
opened for sunlight,
bearer of pitchers,
first water carrier

yet on the raft of your once-living
taken with the torrent
to the deep wells of men,
like the others which followed.

IV

But you may enter here
in the brainwells
of your becoming hosts
where the lilac is grown,
the vine cultivated,
the black bee's honey gathered,
in levels not of your choosing
or even your knowing.

When the silence rings in the head
of those who came after,
from belts of familiar forests,
or dreamed in the stream silver
covering your deadflesh eyes,

you shall sing like a ghost
in the head, sarah, returned
from your home shale,
laced between centuries,
your teardrops in mindscapes,
storms and first wanderings
in the nerve stems of old infants.

You brought those with their moonlights,
and mountain lines hazing, to build bridges
over new waters, with cormorant, heron,
loving and giving. This is your daughterhood,
constant, but mary for a day to the pilotless
in the clan-wrath of waters,

blood memory in the red dawn
of kneeling travellers.

In whispering compass winds
will they see your high jumping form,
starlooking face in old nights
of the flesh of the willmaker.
Rock of the high-plain anthropos,
in whose mind, the fire and the cave,
the high climbing ones in the trees,
the homing to earth. You,

the little red starter.

CARACTACUS IN OXFORD STREET

A strange sector, this greying country
south of the Trinovant, small rushing wheels
carrying the uncloaked in metal chariots,
crouched darkly without beards, or horses
to snort in air, hoof the ground in victory.
Not a rock to be seen, the boundary stakeless
between tribal kinglets, nothing to ring
around cattle or prisoners; only the roar
of axles and metal movers, the shouting
of women, scented and out of the camps,
better used to scour the dust-filled fords
or pile up defences, not one with a water-pot,
legs covered with man-cloth, thin and pale.
The women were stronger in my time,
with short lusty legs, carriers of grain
in large sacks, their children happy
and glad for the sun.

Entries for enemies gape at every passage,
the guards asleep or leaning on hut sides
or talking to comrades; none on roofs
with boulders to roll. The food is chaff
on plates for infants. Where are the sides
of meat, the shaking of spears in the halls
of the Mighty Ones, the gods of the hearth?

CUNOBELINE'S SUNRISE

Now opens this day
with singing birds
rich-headed in trees
by morning causeways
and high larksong
ten centuries of shields
above the horse tracks
and the village barrows
in rising green, the dew
given by the grace
of warrior heavens.
The trance of air
hangs over fighting hills,
– a man's wide arms
might hold as mistress
the golden morning
decked with sweetness
of flower and blossom
until camp chatter
breaks, destroys.

Until the cooking smoke
ascends, and, set for blood,
the chariot knives appear,
the carnyx handled proudly
from its night-hut.

Here ghosts of battle-fathers
fallen, who gave all their sunsets
for these mornings, their bones
for joy like this – a king's sunrise.

GREY

A fine hunting dog, my Grey,
I dug into the foreign strip
far from his home lough
my grieving face low
and over bracken
covering his still blood.

Pain not of my limbs
entered my eyes,
Straightened, I remembered,
Sholan would have made words
for him, for me, crystal
with steady comfort,
blessing his dead-eyes-under
now empty and shuttered,
his bounding trust broken
by a hound of two legs.

May cattle herds and crops
around the throne of *Dis Pater*
renew his mind. The hound-whelp
Fail Inis shall teach him to catch
the great cat Irusan. His mother
will welcome him; fast on four legs
may he awaken to trackers and handlers.

I am leaving the *vicus*, my new home
near the signal station,
the Wall will need me no more,
may the *Limes* break
with the tribes' thundering,
may the Tungrian of the granary
who speared my grey dog
rot with the maggots I delivered him to.

VEDICA

The lady at Ilkley has her hair in plaits,
accurately woven with the skill of a matron
of thirty. Someone remembered her well,
this Vedica, set up her ample form
like a wigged judge - some presider
and no pale beauty. To guess at her
might demean or increase her stature.
If a camp-follower, she was no vacant slut
but a tidy one who knew of her body
like a book, carefully loaned,
when it was due for return,
the cost of the loan to the club member,
if it was taken out. Could it be renewed?
- what about wear and tear - torn cover?
Who chiselled her at death,
one lover, or several - cloaked chief
some night guard besotted by favours
making repayment? her children?
some tribune who married a Roman wife,
deserting a Celtic Butterfly, in his remorse?
Did she die by the singular stroke
of a selfish admirer, whose lips
and no other's might winter above her head,
make whisper his close summer secrets
- a message train islanded only for her,
wafted from flesh on blood-warmed air
before the first *tuba* sounded a killing
to be done, all sweetest moments left
in the charring of love by hate
in a cruel killing wind?
Was she mother and mistress
to six gnarled centurions,
or did she sell wine to layers of *agger*,
receive the *stipendium*, clean the *gladius*,
settle magic of herbs on cuts?

NOTE. The tombstone of Vedica, a Cornovian tribeswoman, was found at Ilkley outside her territory. She was said to be thirty years old. Her hair was in two long plaits. She may have been an ordinary camp follower but more likely was an important or favoured member of the military community.

PETRONIUS

Petronius of the Fourteenth
bore his last standard at Wroxeter,
knew of the Wrekin firing,
trapped blood and screams
from Virico's fortress;
fought for established regime,
containment of Caractacus
of the tribal Royal House
by the Scapula line
of eastern Sabrina.

Legion gods, victory makers,
would lead the long rudders
to sceptre triumph
beyond *Fretum Gallicum*.
in these savage boundaries.

Men trusted the *Genius*,
Imperial guide from Calabria to Venetia,
and the power of the melon bead.

Not at Rutupiae the final Pilot,
but Viriconium, so far from Vicenza
and its life-giving sun, the Juno girls
laughing by lakeside trees.

In this land of rock, mist and rain,
there was a new anniversary
– red blood drawn by *pilum*
in the first foray, spilled tribal gold,
the death tracks of wounded
fleeing from horror at their backs
– so many less for the Thracian horse
to trample, for the kinglets
trying to break the path to Bravonium.

A-17

Some were faithful to Rome,
servants, carriers, sellers of honey,
but would *they* enter Tartarus,
survive without grape wine,
like all trained soldiers?

NOTE. Line 18, 'melon bead': usually a blue glass bead, used by soldiers as an amulet. The tombstone of Marcus Petronius, a standard-bearer of the Fourteenth Legion, was found at *Viriconium* (Wroxeter). This legion had been moved north from *Manduessum* (Mancetter) into the territory of the *Cornovii* to contain the forays of the Welsh tribes and to protect the southwestern route to what is now Herefordshire.

THE LAST STAND OF CARADOG

In years, four hand-fingers since,
was I boy in the Triple Dyke[1],
now in this Siluria my father
Blessed King, or *Brenhan*[2],
was High Druid – *Cynfelyn*, Hound of God
in Prydain, true lord of *Camulodunum*.
Dead my father and loyal brother, the other
fled to Gaius. We left the easterners,
eleven coward chieftains, each sworn to Claudius,
regrouped west. Vespasian rushed us
from the southlands, slingstones unused,
sorned by friends of *Regnenses* and Cogidubn[3],
the false one who opened his land and harbour
to the legions. Some turned north at *Caerfaddon* ,
or at *Caerloyw*, before Scapula blocked the *Hafren*.
Here there are hill-tribes, strongholds
no cavalry reaches, peace for a time,
makers of baskets we used for carriage.

We heard tales from the north route,
where my brother was killed; and from
the *Dumnonii*, of killings by lances and swords,
then slaughter in *Deceangli* valleys through which
we thought to pass. Retreat and advance were cut.
Many dawns my hung cloak shuddered in wind;
voices of messengers always of marching camps
closing the hill-gaps came faster than camp dogs
looking for meat. I moved further north,
the sunrise pointed to forts of the legions
among the *Cornovii*. But the woods were our friends,
the tribes preserved in defeat by the boughs
enclosing their flight. Centurions halted,
soldiers returned to the camps, cutting some down
in the open later, with wives and children.

It was no defeat, nor by the gods a victory.
We went to the stones for guidance,
put trust in signs in the red sand,
the words of two druids of the north
escorted by the hammer fighters[4]
who saw many years of slaying,
the death of Ostorius. I grew impatient,
more raids to the east gained armour, sandals
from outlying posts, an *aureus* or more
for a killer, but no land from the legions.

Why had they come, what need of our huts,
our women, our beads and pots?
Now king of land I did not possess,
I took tribal chiefs and many men
across a river, attacked a camp on the curve,
not far from the mountain pass of its source,
to force a trackway east, well north of the Fosse,
where Romans were less and friends were more.
I sent spies to the south to tell me positions
of cohorts. After three days, when they were close,
I left men to lengthen the trackway, withdrew the rest
up a steep wooded mountain; sent messengers north
while we defended. By Leu[5] and all precious
we held for three days. I travelled the slopes,
encouraging, horses were tumbled and cut
and the riders killed or disarmed
as they fought their way upwards. Again we retreated,
running in lines up a sister mountain.
The Legate's first Century found my family hut,
captured and raped the women. I heard their cries
(would not the Maiden save them from Rome?)
told men to fade into woodland,took thirty northwards
seeking more friends, but finding enchainment.

Sing you then the Land of my Fathers
up in that lark sky overhanging with gods;

dig then the bodies of soulmen, course their blood
in your feeling hearts. Do not forget,
in two millennia you will need their ghosts
to spear passage for country.
Though you be fifty fold,
a tyrant is a bad giant.

1. Catuvellaunian triple-earthwork defences of Cunobelinus, near his capital at Colchester, at Sheepen Farm.

2. The legendary Bran the Blessed.

3. 'King' Cogidubnus, traitor, chieftain in Sussex, who probably allowed the Romans invasion entry on his coasts and other favours at the time of the Conquest.

4. Possibly the name for the Ordovices north of the Silures, handed down from earlier times when that tribe used the stone axe in combat.

5. Lleu. Welsh equivalent of the better known Celtic god Lugh or Lugus, referred to as the Gaulish Mercury by Caesar, hence patron of arts and crafts. A solar deity which a responsible ruler such as Caractacus (Caradog) would call on in the interests of his people. Diminished as time passed to 'Lugh-chromain', meaning 'little stooping Lugh', anglicized as 'leprechaun'.

CORPSE

Uplever her night bones slowly,
expose them to lightning flash;
trowel her maid-crystal gently
under the burial ash.

Here clings her matrix mould,
worm-pierced, run with white root;
the powder of blackwire hair
dry death on each living shoot.

The plough has lifted the message
of the faceless spine to the lark,
crushing her femurs, surrendered
as if to a ghost from the park.

REMEMBRANCE AT THE R.A.F. MEMORIAL, RUNNYMEDE

Poppies and evergreens below the window lights
placed love-handed by widows and mothers,
slowly, as if each second were sacred, for names
long lost to the world; by others - war sweethearts,
now grey, tears grown in their eyes
like evening raindrops discovered gentle -
all brightness now gone from their hair,
once golden, spread over firm shoulders
in those wordless moments, in the pause
at the end of that last leave taken.

Margaret reads the name of he who fathered her child;
Elizabeth, who lost her air-tall son, lives still
with his nursery roses, climbing the mornings
before his final limbs climbed into the Spitfire,
still hears in her head his voice in the choir,
fifteen years young, sees the green and white glass
to the east shone with Jesus.

Here, in the peace, the chosen words -
Per Ardua Ad Astra, the placings of flowers
by the two frail women, solitaries,
spanning the distance to a heaven's memory.
Here the release of thoughts, pure as that light
which strikes the high blossom from a flowering cherry.

FOR MARY (lost April 5th, 1988)

Her beating heart in atoms lies,
so freedom lives when freedom dies.
When moment cannot lengthen day
the pastel flesh must fade away
and leave her friends to agonise.

All flowers decay where stems arise,
the fragrance passes and it's wise
to know a rose can never stay
                                    – like Mary.

That body, which was soul's disguise,
the darting flames will carbonise.
My loss the thought that, though I pray,
I miss the words no voice can say,
no mouth can form, no lips devise
                                    – like Mary.

THE PERMANENCE OF ILLUSION

Roses spring red in gardens,
small girls laugh as they swing,
swung to the light like pardons
for thinking God ends everything.

The pain of remembrance is last
as years flicker by behind strobes,
with all the illusions of ever.
Time moves in his black robes
and corpses play well in the past.

Friends of the times once moving,
are trapped in emulsion in trance,
caught in the moment of proving
the rest of their camera dance.

Corpses play well in the past.
Time moves in his black robes.
With all the illusions of ever,
years flicker by behind strobes,
and the pain of remembrance is last.

THE STEVENAGE WILL

To my serving-men, cots for their lives.
To Thomas and Edward, my sones,
all my guns, dags and knives
and to have from my cellar three tuns
of good liquor. My Holding to John
and my donkey in Bedwell Field
(or he take a French wife and be gonne).
To old Brown my grete hanging Shield,
a fine pair of foals and some hosen.
To Edmund, stout friend, the grey mare,
six and eightpence, a cushion, a dozen
fat pigeons. A mattress of hair
for my nurse, a strong chest and loom,
my swete *Psalms* – long may she broodeth.
To Robert, good servant, a room
with a window. My best cow to Judith.
For Susan, ten roods of my hides
at Wymundsley, a clock and a cloathe
to soften the saddle she rides.
To my Wife and Companion both,
the Orchard at Stonny-Croft Gate,
the rents from my Messuage at Cromer
(less debts, whether early or late
to be paid). My leathern-bound Homer
to Ben. To William the Parson,
ten pounds for the poor box, a goblet
of silver, two books for his children.
To Percival Gravley a doublet,
some coloured silk in a bale,
a long-handled shovel for bread.

Ten Stalls in Stanmer with Ale
that all drink to my health when I'm dead!

The Infiltrations

ATTENTION DIES AS HARD AS A HORSE BATTERY
(an after-television experience)

Mind's neurals, trained to measure
externals, always react to visions
in commercial mode; when high wands
wave in society by television, other media,
to gain attention by professional magic.
Imprisoned dreams, silent starved thoughts,
cannot free their realities when under the will.
No body self-saves, the life of the gadget,
screen, impositions, are too strong
in demanding attention.

States of first sleep sometimes suffer
mental pollution, attention dies slowly,
maniac cells still live in disturbance
when whiteness of mind is upon us.
Highwaymen of synapses brandish
their pistols, demi-culverins roar
across sensitive cortical marshes.

So even in half-sleep, before REM,
voracious nerve endings quickly react
to imprints of *Dad's Army, The Street,*
to frenzies of angled guitars, writhing tarts,
all possible shots of camera crews,
'soaps' for all seasons. All produce gremlins
 - thrown darts at the mind's soft parts,
spoiling the ichor of any new Eden.
Appetites drift and diminish quite slowly.

Attention dies as hard as a horse battery
as the night-chair teases my vertebrae,
reminds of bed, with a Horlicks ......

Seeped in from Brussels is the Ball
of the Duchess of Richmond, curtseying,
fanning its way through the chattering morse
of still unremorseful 'commercials'.
In the half-darkened brain, redcoats
sweep in from flanks; on the pillow crest
cannons are ready, lines of skirmishers
zoom in and retreat; the window moonlight
threads the lace curtains, in adventure
of rays, like silver musket shot.

Downbed is the upper half of His Grace
on Copenhagen screened by the footboard
bobbing his black cockade, telescope
drawn for sighting. Yes, yes, By Sabre!
Wellington, I see Your Grace, Sir,
Tell your picquets to howitzer mailshots
to fall like napoleons, fluttering
on the hall carpet two hours after dawn;
the 95th Rifles to pepper the postman's trousers,
the Heavies to trample the signs of digestion
in all *Reader's Digest* communiqués;
order the Brunswickers to cut all the lines
of magnetic forces, of clocks, telephones,
alarms, door chimes and all sleep rousers.
Yes, By Sabre! I hear you well, 15-tog high
on the duvet of your Waterloo. Anglesey,
Your Grace, shall tell us again "By God Sir,
I've lost my leg!" And then you will answer
"By God, Sir, so you have!"

At first light, riders from Mons,
gallop their time-slips under my pupils;
woods green in, under my cheek; a gaggle
of generals exposed to the enemy attract
five adventures of cannon balls. Cuirassiers
charge from Nivelle; a brigade bivouaced

under my bolster awakens to a bugle
of sparrows disturbing some batteries
which limber to horses, rattling to Wavre
behind my ear lobes, plunging down ridges
of auricular danger. Even my eyelids
are traversed by Ney's infantry.
Roundshot from Blucher ricochets
from eyelash to nostril ....

Then oversounding, the ring and the ring
of the unlimbering on my doorstep
of the milkman's casket.
The rose on the ceiling commands attention
where casques once bobbed, thick as princes.
The tensions of Monday morning
with its sights, sounds, movements
are stronger than Wellington.
Attention dies as hard as a horse-battery!

AND LIFE HAS NO DOMINION

Formless transparencies glide with no passion
through corpuscular flesh, solid in fashion,
trailing time-corridors, biological tunnels;
sized and unsized, hood high and hem low,
imprinting pallidly footshapes, the glow

of hands on a blood-vessel wall, timed
within a white second. Nerve fibre, limed
with gross messages, dulled by the drumbeat
of outer enormities, pan-roar of air,
detects nothing infaced, more silent than bare

water lapping. Flesh avidly bummng the land,
strawburning events in the brain, is only the grand
transformer to faeces of available fuel.
Midsummer sports, yielding sweat to the crevices,
sense no intrusion from ghosts with their heresies.

Known in chosen crepuscular moments when fluids
quieten, or nurtured in groves by avuncular druids,
ghosts spin and flute invisible ways in human tissue
where self-puppetry offers no godpath or vital strains
but only inwebs asylums of jumping Janes

and Johns, concatenations of torsoed events, way
before arks were cubitted. Life's lost dominions may
entrance, exit, jostling cells meet in their synagogues
dazed in their passions, their sunsets and dawns
successions of memories of mist-vanishing lawns.

Ghosts think no food or sex, express no opinions;
the dead leave their chromosomes - ghosts,
silent as lakes, then form their dominions.

DEATH WAS NO EMPTY HAT

Death was no empty hat, but a swung trapeze
    swept through a hall of song.
Hung on a silver wire, the winging bar
    leaped in a singing breeze.
Riding with woe, the sweet violins of home
    grieved in the high wall-lilac,
and the cadences of a shadowless piper called
    piteously from old pavements.

I heard, with the sighs of centuries, pagan notes
    whispering in the cupola,
and saw, in the flare of thunderhooks, scarecrow skies
    with wondering savage moons,
and a horn with flag ribbons blown by a coloured bird
    flying before my eyes.

AGES UNTO AGES

White sing the living at evensong
where sounded the tones of the musical dead,
for the night stones bred the ghost-high aura
which bounded the clerestory over their bed.

Heaven was where the ancients spoke,
hell, the inversion of earth-green things;
waxen the faces where blood-life flowed
– God's marionettes on artery strings.

For souls of the bodies of children and children,
limp where unfiltered moonlight wanes,
long was the sleep but longer the learning
until under new mothers' counterpanes.

TIN-RIVER GHOSTS

Quiet buddha minds
breathe continuums;
others, karmas unaccepted,
use brains as battering tools
at life's hard rockface,
hustle clefts with metal blows,
smelt veins of discontent,
cause tin-river ghosts to flow,
thought forms aping their creators.

Tin-river shells, androidal, stand
in cloaked dominions, statue-nodes
stretched between the astral poles,
metallic on their risen levels
of harsh repeater-beacon sands
confronting the release from flesh
in the dark night of the soul.

Tin-river ghosts, casque-empty
Modreds, threaten extinction
of the Light beyond the Wheel;
gonfalons expose the writings
of the laws of multi-death.
Poised, pre-shaped, they confront
their makers' minds, risen
from their squat of earth.
And yet time-counting phantoms
vanish to overlands, discredited
tin-lilies, should guelder roses
as love's symbols, appear in stillness
lining a companion path,
leading Arthur-seeking souls
to final Avalon.

Emotion's tin – cast off
like sound reverberating
and reviving, sister copies,
clones of high lust or love,
secret ecstacy, one-day gladness,
or an hour of hatred – thought wishes,
they gather all, tin phantoms
of the coat of personality.

Poet and peasant stand their blessings
or their evils here – tin-river fragments
of their living, all energy conserved,
where stretch the hunting grounds
beyond the molecules of flesh,
the dross on one bank, the Styx
between it and their own creations,
the skiff of truth aligned with metal dolls
their own earth-systems cast.

NOTES

"Light beyond the Wheel": on the Tree of Life the soul may progress to the
Wheel of Fortune. It is here that it might not go further and be denied the 'light'
of the higher sephiroth. It may return on the Wheel to its starting point,
through imperfections, and need to relearn in more physical bodies.

Arthur and Avalon here must be seen in the context of champion of highest
religious principles and the final abode of perfection, respectively.

CENTURY HOUSE

The five-age walls feel the wind from blue waters
overhung in the cool witch-chimney,
and the ghost heart of a summer-wife, waking,
has recalled the sleepy fables
told all to the sun and her cradled daughters,
and how there was gold on the breast of a swanbird
when she sang to the river children.

She remembers the Easter firefly kisses
dancing from his dear lips,
and the two of them in the early shadows,
waiting bold as Welsh fairies
for moonlight over the dark home hills.
She has replaced the growing thorns
with roses of yesterday;
white as the leading phantom petals
she smiles through palace years,
and the wind from blue waters steals
to the thrush for her homely garden voice
– to the sundial for her tears.

THE OLD OAK

Rafters enclose caught beauty,
core wood computes the touch mutely
of dear friends, emotions now ceased,
the record of goodness released
from old times. Some entered, embraced
by old timbers, took meals and graced
a room for a night, well framed
with hostelry wood, to be named
in sap-dry receptors, open, benign
to the magic of friendship, the sign
of the human blessed with the bloom
of driven blood, foreign to doom
by the tree saw, loss of vegetal soul.
With atmosphere flooding the bowl
of man's spirit, the old oak takes it all,
remembers, records, releases at call
of like minds, infusing the air.

Yet dislikes the brush and the hair
of puppies when restless, rank scents
of perfume, the nudging advents
of bluebottles. All cats soon tingle
from wood-borne ghosts, they single
out movements, recorded as strange;
neural codes, not of humans, but the range
beyond claws, so they rest undismayed,
although curious. These ghosts maybe trade
in mice, so they notice and wait
for energised wainscotings to offer this bait.

Strides of the long grain bear the stress
of sap years and dry years, in timelessness.
Here the green triumph, revival in death,
good company pulsed in the old oak's breath.

OLD FRAGRANCE

Halting and walking in strange dead seasons,
through the weak lights of ghost Octobers,
surrendered to the final lute,
they sing from melodies unborn:

they have chanted how they remembered
the first sleeping diamonds of dew
on the white flowers left weeping
by the wall, in the graveyard dawn;

they have forgotten that instant without breath
in the green, midnight glory of cool ferns
– that moment in the lonely bedroom
when a whole heart sighed through curled fingers
and passed between two winds in the corn.

TRANSMIGRATION OF SOUL

That raven's my sister
on the sky-corner seat
of the man building sited
near old George the Fifth
tramlines.

The morning's her mind hour
of memory roses, fleet
two-footed trespass through
gates of unfeathered
farmers.

Air-queen of summer,
I salute her on wing,
oversailing my garden
and my church's sad empire
of prayers.

ASHRAM

Thought was almost a wave-form,
an elusive violet
beamed from internal antennae;
western truths were without substance.

It was the way of non-violence;
the spirit was on their faces,
sun in their empty shoes,
the spinning-wheel ... a symbol.

THE DREAM-CATCHER

The magic of dreams,
events timed in curious collects
of running images
is a secret sleep process
with illogical laws
unexplained on awakening.
The direction of Man,
roped superconscious
to arguments, rights of the tribe,
rewound in increasing neurosis,
needs the succour of dream-making.
Destiny is in the brain as it sleeps,
when protected from harlequin struggle.

Shamans who knew the birds of the air
which came from the whirling image,
the sacred earth, made the catcher,
keeping the sleeper from harm.
passing the strengths of the night,
passing not spirits of evil
– a fire-fence against faces, bodies
reaching the soul's dark night
through the inconstant fog;
repelling the parchment ghosts
building on silent pillow, alchemies
of Qliphoth at the level of chaos.
Crimson and white, the tasselled grid
screened the dreamer, confronted
verandahs of elementals, saved
for the dawn the strengthening
parts of dream, the solar levels
helpful for the tribe's new day.

NOTE. The dream-catcher was a tasselled network hung above the sleeper, used
by North American Indians as a protection while he/she was dreaming.

THE INTEGRATION

In middle blue,
the facemaster of arrows,
stone-cast phantom
of the castle precinct,
rides orders to six pale archers
of the gift, suspended snow-work
where clouds roll slowly
through the curtain wall.

Queen of the green square,
his silken lady of the manor
repels her enemies, crude serfs,
collapses bridge-runs, ejects
all knaves from boundaries,
whip-tumbles trespassers
down valley sides.
They fall in minor patterns,
take dominions in new wombs
of earth-brains closed at night
from bright sensation
and inter-neuron calls on body trips
at boating levels, rocking limbs
in seas of tinsel suns,
now forgotten, now unreal.

Fine atomic lips encircle
real frenzies of green park and castle;
mind freespins, transfers
its cone of tumbled fugitives,
its ring of cosmic archers
to sleep-level rhythms; above,
the open town moon floats
above the in-cubed integral,
a dynasty of proud encastled flesh
and arrowed heart.

EXPERIMENTA LUCIFERA

The path unwavering as Luther's,
catechisms alive on woodcuts,
instructive with Bible episodes;
liturgy refreshed with hope-strung music
guiding the Word of God to the human,
air made sacred and outringing
majestically to stir the unsure heathen,
to repel a clinging Satan, who'd flee
from the simple gaiety of Love Divine.

Or, sleeping on some stone Jacobian pillow,
not to dream of the stern God of Abraham
but awaken an inner soul, fire-eyed
cosmic serpent struck from the Mulhadara,
the Fire Kundalini shining like molten gold,
those laddered angels the petalled chakras;
to know on the breath, elemental prana
taken from the wind's four quarters
at that Bethel of the sanctified stone.

Or, monk-like, with cloistered power
to move light along the rubrics,
illuminate the Gospel, glowing,
like the great Book of Lindisfarne,
flowing the Word to the reaching heart;
gentler, quieter, by inward spirit,
skill engaging with scroll and line,
close-holding energy in patterns
ultimate in Celtic purity and tone.

Or travel calmly through angry cities,
to enter and leave doors in service,
to uncover truth in places greedy
for treasure, all-seeking for kingship;
like Gandhi, kindling by peaceful resistance

and high simplicity, spirit of body,
lighting faith in the space of an ashram,
encouraging all in the village harvesting
– all these are designs of gods' callings.

NOTE. There was light before fruit in the Creation. Ways of progress to help
others see the 'Light' are primary to *Experimenta Lucifera*. See Bacon (*Novum
Organum* i, aph.XCIX).

POET AND PAINKILLER

Somewhere in the violet of mind,
a still lake spreads, boundaries
of surface and sediment cut off
by ice lines of pain, razor rims
slicing poet from sustenance
of air, fire, earth, water.

Time moves, leaving small spaces
for guillotined adjectives, hasty phrases,
A poet's tightrope, no manoevres
except by chemical loosening
widening rope to platform
every six hours.

Bless the co-dydramol
for a haiku, a stanza, something
filched by subterfuge from the lake,
some lacuna-spoiled phrase
fished out in haste,
quickly extracted, forced through the ice,
avoiding weed strangulation at birth.

Sleep, if it comes, dawn recollection,
may bring words which bridged
the intractable flesh.

The Worldly Ones

THE OVERWALKING

A catwalk satin venus overwalking
meadowsweet. Doomed dairy day
the moment of this chosen favour
made peasants of field maidens
light in radiant corn; laughs
by swinging boughs outfashioned.

The owl of genesis knows all, sees all
beginnings, advises none. Who tip their ramp,
force-roll their own direction. Perhaps
the catwalk ends where Eves of artifice,
eyes of blinded Adam, find new services,
new bibles of their own where rubrics dim,
die directionless, as scattered embers fade,
over-blackening primal images
of first awakening of flower flesh,
over-shadowing the spirit diamond
of both field and water.

Adventurers all, who pace or race
the crises of the lands, in war
run ambulances, rescuing by bridge
and stretcher, taking downline
flesh tatters still a part of form.
Wars overwalk the jags, the undulations
of the stricken earth. And yet
sunroll and spring may evergreen
some new Hill 60, a once-bloodied ground
- a thrush sit singing, overpeering
where pens for U-boats housed
wolf-packs of oceans. And yet
some tulips grow in Ravensburg,
while mistral winds, white snows, return

as if there never were red crystals
where ambulancières saved men
lying in them, soon overwalked.

Youth traverses, repeats mistakes.
The broken tinder land of colonies
is reworked without direction
of the masters, rough–fledged again.
Drums of thought sound over those
who planned the centuries.
Pantomime frosts and storms recycle,
restage their problems. Man finds
new questions for new answers,
and then new questions;
unrivets rivets, destroys the sowing,
then resows; ends crises with the overtone
of some new crisis;
sees nothing beyond his own footlights,
his overwalking in his time,
each practicality a pragmatism
confronted by another.
He stands enfleshed,
using his exits and his entrances,
in strengths and weaknesses,
his multi–flamens guiding his despairs,
his hopes of lion's gold;
and yet, in years, neutralising
his pale deific power.

Where jasmine bloomed,
or planes reflected stars,
we walk below the zodiacs
of our impermanences.

THE HULKING ON THE MEADOWS

Field emerald reflects luck lightness,
brightness of clasp or hair braid,
rightness of lock and old gods
stood up for manform crowds
straight in the old green places,
connecting planes to humans
seeking suitable transcendence,
platform, or plane of first perspective
in the land decreed.

Hulks destroy, manmade monstrous
monsters, flesh or mineral, usually
with land-flat bases, immovable,
delighting in de-lighting meadows
of fenced green, the silver trails
of god-ideas in the Adam brain.
Yesterday's shine remover,
Tomorrow's permanent impression.

Iron-corpsed giants press heather,
heathen to the end under sanded sites,
big-foot concrete - hulk facets.
Hulk minds bulge fourways, explode
with thought excreta, covering sward,
white field lilies, roads of rose memories,
pale children of first-birded meadows.

Yet from chaos, frequencies of beauty
dismembered, unstrung, heights
of gothics unhung, flesh deterred
by heavy squatting, the spine,
some pillar of solid mystery
can integrate, pre-time another chaos,
If and if only, for race protection.
In the qliphoth is the terraced spirit,

the shaped negative, the defiant ugly,
the starter in the rock.

For in the chaos is the liquid mage,
on the waterfronts of despair, always
but always, the invitation of bells,
the union of events where without reason
is the fitting together of clown and thinker,
where the logical timed event is the illusion.
The path of hulking is removed from grace,
is in destroyed Sunday time,
but in the first cause is the healing,
the putting together, where time itself
is the illusion, and hulking the vain endeavour.

Yet in old timed forests, hominid ground,
the hulking *was* the grace and time the leaf,
the choice was single, grace and hulking
was in the existence and its movements.
The separation was in the activities of thought,
the driver of thumb and forefinger, the decision
to support or destroy the tribe,
the harmony or the hulking
the three million year-choice,
from Lucy to Lucy.

GREAT AUNT CLARA'S LOST MOMENTS

Enter nephews, beard-sprouted,
bored with Adlerian therapy
and old-hat Freudian theory;
– professional discussers in pubs
of the rising and falling of markets,
homo-eroticism, phallic symbols,
post-coital transcendentalism
and the downfall of the monarchy.

Enter nieces (death has scared voices
from buccal embrasures usually unemployed
without parlour lights, television,
masculine cannonball quips),
usually nose-down in qwerty,
high-paid secretarial electronics,
tabset hopes keyed west of Whitehall
amid glorious artifices of workstations
where trained fingers revel.

The empty council flat of Clara
is an atmospheric brake,
no 'Words for Windows' here,
when faced by the death of life –
only windows of Clara without words,
lace-curtained, hall-floor starters
– five bills, eleven free newspapers,
nineteen Daily Mirrors, mailshots
including free pizzas, a special offer
– half-fare for pensioners to Outer Mongolia.

Traditionally, it's time for keening processes
among relatives, actual or *in simulacrum* ,
profitless sentiment, attempts at sadness,
handkerchief production for wetting,
not practised since Clara wore overalls,

did it for real after factory work,
with her dear mother's picture before her,
read all the right things (*Matthew* to *John*,
Hardy, Kingsley, *Arabian Nights*)
to her young sisters and brothers;
paid all the bills without help.

Not that now, all's improved
with hand-outs, euthanasia schemes
to deliver grandparents to God, or
hide them in rest-homes, last-year hours
well tucked away, in pockets of unknowing,
un-interfering with more desirable sequences
of Marbella and gigs, strawberry ices.

Better still, soon, Euro-coffins worldwide
supplied by Saga through the Channel Tunnel.
When great aunts, grandmothers are brown,
leftover leaves in rooms, is need
for efficient sweepings, burnings.
How else continue the party spirit, keep
phallic adventures unwrinkled, the tabloids
profitably sprouting breasts and fashions
for newly initiated humans on the bridge of life?

On unfamiliar ground,
glances askance shot in the hallway
are diverted by a green lavatory brush
doorstopping the bathroom,
not part of the social scene;
inside against its north wall
is an oval bone with magic sigils
engraved (like those in popular astrology
for office girls), flat on a black floor tile
like a Crowleyan apport.
Closer examination defines the object,
(not even as shorthand on Atlantean stone

or pre-Adamite ornamentation)
as a piece of cracked soap last used by Clara.
In the bedroom is a bemattressed TV
ready to keel, left for take away,
No Clara to finger its knob.
A blue-ringed saucer, deserted by cup,
cerulean eye expectant of nothing, hands
no longer there to restore and centre the wanderer,
is chinawise resigned from rim to bottom, ready
to return to its Maker, as stamped
'Foster and Entwistle, Torquay'.

These are unavoidable matters,
minutes with artefacts encountered reluctantly,
supremely unimportant compared with the latest
novelty dresses swishing the catwalks.

They have their moments, who electrify
reactive wires nerving through blood
with the ghosts of absence.
A strangeness covers each wall plane
and object, an invisible dustsheet
defies the fingertips to undertouch.
- a spell soon broken but impressing many
to fly for fortitude to city limits,
where vectorially friendly pavements,
buildings of rational dimensions, even
the doubtful security of sandwich bars
give some mortal relief.

Meanwhile, with bravados of superior
solid weapons, freeholders of the firescape,
down at the Council Dump, fire gas jets
to finger around photograph corners,
send to Vulcan memories of picnics,
Sunday lands inhabited by long dresses,
large hats, waterborne punts, croquet,

Margate pier, sea scenes, a small Clara paddling;
reduce a panorama of three and a half donkeys
into charred curly paper. Remorseless
pressurised mini-*flammenwerfers*
blacken, seethe victories of destruction
over images foreign to torso-hells
of all incinerators gainfully employed.

Her empty flat shell is
rewhitened, rewashered, re-allotted,
re-enlisted for families. A minefield
of slumbering infants displaces silence.
Disturbed by the new day, they run,
new heroes trooping under paper hats,
whooping after lemonade, capering
to glory like eager generals, like death
has no dominon, to MacDonalds, like
memory's new seedlets in their birthday light,
like croquet games that never were,
like no great aunts.

HIGHER THAN A CEPHALOPOD
(lines to a materialist)

I   state no more than your sinews
will believe, their connections
to what evolved in your blastula
dividing from conjunction
in the July heat;

a feat not dissimilar to aftermaths
of coupling of sentient monkeys
extrapolated from Darwin,
resulting also in divisions
of hunter and prey.

Gay in your unreal world of light years
(distances, not time),
seasons of movements and smells
(sun angles, not time)
your truths are your waistcoat watch,

the snatch of seconds to stuff
pizzas in your sac, undo your flies,
anything living, with these processes,
physical, meat pushing or pulling,
anything that, ceasing movement, dies.

Rise, knight of cells,
statement of a cosmic god,
reality veiled, fortune
lower than your bloodaxed angel,
higher than a cephalopod.

THE DONOR OF THE OASES

After crust-ripping bombs,
wild death parties
facing the unfaceable,
the tenth cyclonic war-wind
in disturbed air,
a calm came to pass.

Bearing pole-clubs, behammering,
some gathered rock chippings
from embrasures, dropout districts,
splinters of mock alabaster,
oddments, which ground,
blood-wetted from the dead,
would form a nutritional matrix
for close-planted mushrooms
grown under stars. in night holes,
while the hung dust cleared.

Others, armour not sweated on
for pelvic protection, removed it,
waded to the island women
through bio-scums and belly-up fish,
animal dung, debris of a country museum
floating, found a hand assassinated at wrist.
Rooted to palm, still labelled,
some curator's symbol of silent resistance
– a last specimen: "*Gramineae* (grass)".

We had feared, now would be rain, we hoped,
tears of thankfulness under new suns,
grandchildren on refruited land.
So it was we made a replanting
for mushrooms, green oases in terrible wastes.
And in faith resprung from the symbol given,
hoped for new springs from a severed hand.

THE DIVINE IMPALERS

Staked bodies perish in fires
of lawful Golgothas. Torch and knife targets
destroyed by the wills of true believers,
justice fighters, Robespierres and others,
have withered the centuries. In His name
humans arranged the high faggots,
burned witches, engined swords through the guts
of innocent Cathars; honour flown
when Lear's was the kingdom
ripe for the taking. Even at Agincourt
our good Henry prayed for an hour,
knowing his archers set behind stakes
would encourage impaling.

O Lord, give us Victory,
if God's will yield a Calais,
all's right in the world.

THE CRUSHING IN THE PRIORY OF SAINT BARTHOLOMEW

Raherius, know wickedness cruelly wrought
in thy building holy to Bartholomew's name,
on land sought piously from Henry, king,
at Smoedfeld: therefore for this
we sorrow poor mortals, let the bell ring
Sancte Petre Ora Pro Nobis.

This bloody deed, with devil's work fraught
in the Church of the Butchers, is now the shame
of Canterbury, done by no underling
but the Crossbearer: therefore for this
we sorrow, poor mortals, let the bell ring
Sancte Johanne Baptiste Ora Pro Nobis.

Bullying Boniface, that priest untaught,
Archbishop in Ordinary entered, to maim
the faithful sub-prior, in armour to fling
and to crush: therefore for this
we sorrow, poor mortals, let the bell ring
Sancte Bartholemeo Ora Pro Nobis.

NOTE: Raherius or Rahere, king's jester and musician, after pilgrimage to Rome
where St. Bartholomew appeared in a dream, is related to have obtained land at
Smithfield from Henry I. On it, the church and famous hospital were founded in
1123 A.D. The church is the oldest one in a London parish. Sometime in 1150
A.D., Archbishop Boniface, wearing armour under his robes, entered uninvited,
crushing the elderly sub-prior against a choir stall, breaking his bones and
causing other damage. The inscriptions on three of the remaining pre-Reformation
bells are given at the end of each verse of the poem. The treble bell was
dedicated to the Saint.

SALESPERSON

The chatter performance, prime wordage,
gasconades of superlatives, gush out
to North Finchley housewives. The podium
is hers, the stadium the bargain basement.

High voltage adjectives short-circuit the ears;
the brain is fused immediately, causing
immobility in the voluntary muscles
of the standing audience, but freed
to release the wrists to sign cheques,
open purses. Monetary drive
knows no boundaries.

She's not so tireless.
Though her mouth in full phrase
is a healthy panoramic ellipse,
it reverts to a slanting rhombus
at the end of each eulogy
of eastern promise for a new scent
to attract good-time males
west of the Marylebone Road.
Through the miasma of her persuasions,
his muscular legs appear on dream verandahs
trailing with pheremonal florescence.

One wonders, when home, if she screams
"pass the pickle!" or under the sales talk
is as sweet as bryony on a south wall;
or is she a special – the seventh daughter
of a seventh daughter; even some throwback
aping the legendary mitochondrial Eve,
an African who once traded bargain berries
for beads paid in by simple itinerant hominids?

IN PRAISE OF CUSHIONS

Cushions are velvet visions
sunken for love in the evening,
or plunked into rows of dromedaries
for the social occasion.

Thrown between spouses in sport,
they simulate earthy pummelling,
putting brakes on the higher self
which is needed to disappear.

In their yielding turgidities,
their unctious, adaptable moulds
for rump against rump, is the frame
for a bum-humming paradise.

Magic Moments

THE WHITE RIVER

In his dream he was again a shaking boy,
a sail blown on luminous waters,
a winking wraith following a white river
unwinding to an open jetty,
finding a vessel like a green thief

lying curiously in the shallows,
and a pale girl kneeling beside,
a playmate from the avenue of flowers
calling quietly along the white river
his forgotten name.

There was venom in the woman of wood
rising grey-handed from wind wilderness,
claiming his life and his small voice;
but the girl held out a prism of glass,
and in it he left two silver stars,

brothers to his twin young eyes,
while she flung roses rich as blood
into the ferry tide, to float with him
in the white river
for ever.

GREAT AUNT IN MACDONALDS

Here, with two shopping bags,
A Great Aunt sits in Macdonalds,
lifting a complimentary coffee
to lips which kissed a Great Uncle
in a carriage in the Age of Steam.

Undisturbed by the outré pants
of anti-Augustans reading tabloids
or multiple imminence of infants
thrashing their limbs, only pigeons
taking off or alighting in the Square,
oblivious to anything three inches or more
above their arbitrary pecking zones,
demand her unmoving attention.

GEOMANTIC LOVE

Love within love
unspoken for, she comes
to my quiet breath;

drops mantle in silence
by a circle of water,
ch'i of paths;

faces east on tiger ground
where the blue dragon bears me,
in pressure of blood.

White ferns, hill arms
know of the double mating

– magic foreign to cities
brightens the wind.

NOTE. Places for fortunate living in China are where 'blue dragon' male topography adjoin 'white tiger' female topography. If there is also human love in these places, the concept of 'double mating' both of man and nature can be entertained.

RIVA

She is my night body,
forest sleep-flower
with red sap, black hair
on green moss-pillow,
deserving beads,
protective amulets
for waking moments.

Her name is Riva,
always this her mouth
forms into words
in thanks for summer gold,
my gifts of stones from the plain,
bark from the tribal tree,
the serpent ring,
my knot of green leaves
on the grey wall
where her head rests.

Her strange white bird
always comes for her corn
-a feathered hunter
on Riva's ground
looking two ways.

This sun day
after she wakes
I will leave her
with cooking fish,
run to my mother's
water home,
bring her back
tiger coral
like a god's present.

THE CAVE

The cave was sweet at the end,
wild herbs on the oxhide,
flowers strewn by hands truer
to move to the transference
of a god's tear to humanity
of the ancients of ages
than Victorian palms
put together for Jesus.

She would follow her hunter,
make for his children and hers
a place for lying, an entrance
open and green. his weapons
protecting her body and his;
his mouth of rough honey
her right of possession
flown in through the window of stars.

THE DREAM OF THE PRIMITIVE

Sounds of bird and beast
were part of him,
useful personal registers
of place, area, space,
signalling danger or food,
in his dream of living.
Depending on the event,
he went towards or away
from the signal's direction.

Once, for some reason,
the sun was bright over lake water
near summer-bush scent,
and he appeared to himself,
made his mirror arm move,
seem to catch fish
with a hand grasping air;
forgot, in the urge of season
with this dream long in mind,
that this was unusual.

But in frost time
the dream became broken;
despair cried in his limbs,
pain pressed on his eyes.
There was a loss, inevitably,
a shock fusing the network,
the system of animal thought,
in exchange for control
gained over the elements
air, earth, water, fire.
Finding his wandering girl-child
face down and dead in the snow
was that human moment
timing the point of awakening.

AMULETS

Amulets hold practice of mind
firm to their might, enwrap, bind
against dark forces grouping to spear
the psychic porphyry, reflect fear

in proportion to belief grown
freely in their working – stone,
six-pointed star, Davidian; shell
from holy pool, corded bell;

signs, sigils, numbers; bark
from sacred trees, tablets; mark
against evil, moon-reared plant
– as atoms, common shapes, grant

they no favour until, streamed in a faith,
the inner white blood flows, the wraith
of all structures, invoked, lends mystery
to amulets, guardians through history,

consistently hallowed, with faith's white
core, god-forms usurping protocol's right
sense effects of hue, form or weight
– the wearer a king, all evil a state

of impotence. More faith lights more vectors
directed from amulets, enswords these protectors.

INSIDE *THALASSUS MARINUS* **

Mine eye, my mind
a dynamite point
born with blue streamers
depth encapsulated on silicon,
oxygen cargoes ring my lake.

Pelican-winged I visited four
overmoving my Order, further,
carried on dream slivers of foam,
to coasts of six sides, white ferns fringing,
shifting in winds of three moments.

Above and below a vertical alley-light
filters the rifts. As if it were green water,
smoothed for sliding to base, also
as if mind could be pointed and turned
upwards to pure blue sky. Here,
spaces in time concentrate energy,
trojan patterns, for resting and blessing.
So be violet my mind in this lattice,
almost a room, almost a universe
of sky and sea, land in space
winged by side gratings, film-thin
fleets of pale ships on the floor,
sky-raiders in ice clouds above
my mind.

Poet of immediate terrors,
I have had strange mistresses,
none more than the invitations
to wombs of molecules,
in lined passages of rigid
playmate dolls, arm and leg
to arm and leg. In my flesh,
its secondary space and existence,

too simple in the endurance of crystal,
one sea, one sky, one lesser life,
is my incompleteness.
I am not yet made.

** One name for the aquamarine crystal.

THE MAIDEN OF THE MOON'S BOAT

Behind these yellow leaves I see the maiden of the moon's boat,
her smile straying, her light throat bent over the path of
suffering.
Inside a convent of trees she rides, the Bride of my God,
floating a silver mile below her shining side,
as I, like these many branches, open my heart to her.

The Flip Side

TURNING

Turning
in the child's eye
it patrols four blue corners;
a beautiful vision
with no name
created from pure thought,
an airship of the mind.

Thoughts are reality,
patrolling many corners,
like turning airships.
Circus mares
obey their ringmasters,
turning to the whip.

The man in the three-cornered hat
turns his head slowly to the right.
and then downwards.
He is a highwayman
on a horse under a tree
expecting the Royal Mail,
then inspecting his pistol
which gleams in the moonlight.

The man with the newspaper
held before his eyes
reading the stockmarket report
is not going straight to his office.
He is on a seat in a Circle train
which curves to the left.
Getting out, he has executed
an eighty-six degree turn.

STANDING ON A POINT

Standing on a point, it could be anywhere
my lungs received oxygen, my army boots
were Gulliverian, legs shrunk to lines,
the sun unreflected from mirror to eye
with no angels to create draughts.

Nothing to distract – perhaps at night
on a canine in the Natural History Museum
belonging to a small dinosaur, the vibrations
of conducted school parties long gone, leaving
just a snicker or two from the astral, and
the ghost of a former curator, somewhere
west of the ammonites, quite harmless.

It's temporary toothland – blood, sweat,
liquids of the night, used shaving water
at dawn, will drain down the throat of whatever
was once a force in the Upper Cretaceous.

Of course, there is much to stand on, needles,
the ends of ready-sharpened pencils (Woolworths),
stalagmites, the dorsal hairs of fox-terriers.
I could go on, but I've made my point.
You must experiment with skewers, rose thorns,
wands clenched by determined Christmas fairies,
the upturned moustaches of capitalists.
I would not pin you down.
But wait for the darkness.

DIAL A DANCE, TWENTY-SIXTH CENTURY

It's an Olde Time dance, the Jackson Lift,
spun and fisted now by the near-demised
for five-hundred years. Over to Greta, shift
the leading to her as I twist left her anodised
navel to 'seven', then back to the right ('fifteen'),
adjusting the 'mode' and 'rate', with her feet
at a cruising angle. Her body has been
set for a trip on the dancing-iron sheet;
force 'twelve' for power and adhesion (a rich
combination); then electro-perfection of style
by throwing her underarm switch.
Left hand on Greta's cold hip, right hand on dial
in her scapula, I turn it for 'strong aromatics'.
The music starts – heavenly peach-blossom spray
follows our dance pattern as she jerks me away.

NEAR-DEATH EXPERIENCE FOR ALFRED IN THE KITCHEN

Alfred, a stroke-rigid, is about to part jump
in pre-ambulance time, the other part, thought-drained
is held by Dorothea stapled to her kitchen apron,
(which is what it gets through helping with the washing-up).
Electric daylight pulls the first part four-square
out to the great earth retina which sees all, guides all
beyond the soul-blasted window frame.
Behind, all pink nose and tears on six sides,
Dorothea recedes to fleshdice with a red dishcloth
cruppered on the two-face.It's a gamble, he takes the light tunnel
running through his cabbage patch to a foreign end
clasping a moving funicular ribbonlight. Outside, an eject,
its a golden ocean with sun dwarfs trailing astral strands
across the waves, else a Jackson Pollock cosmobilia
forgotten floataway.

Thinks fireship in reverse and apple-trees,
gains land and Sunday beachlight, rope winds curling,
aromatic, beyond the trees a dwelling of faces
remembered, Gran, and Jonesey with facelines of 37 bus wheel.

Shocked, hooks back to atomic hold, still lawful,
trees fade, forces rag him back against the tunnel wall,
like pain, like breath against a carrot grater,
like nose in hissing trap of oxygen – a ward of light
above the leaning face of undiced Dorothea.

THE TRANSFORMATION OF THE LESBIAN RHOMBUS

The Mother of all Green Rhombuses
slews her sides down Pyramid Mountain,
angles and all, a female Incredible Hulk
in two dimensions – a waterless
slut uncramping her oriform lust.

In a perfect cave at the base
leased from a subdivided polygram
of polythalamous tendencies,
a female blue square, small
but chunky, breakfasts innocently
on ovals, line stalks, trochocephalic titbits,
curvilinear chocolate thins
and pantomorphic jelly babies.

She does not know
the Green Rhombus is a lesbian
of many-sided appetite
(looking for blue squares
in cylindrical caves without
bicornate protection or
arcuate secret weapons)
capable of tetragrammic collapse
to force entry into mountain holes
of any dimension –
a multilateral mugger capable
of the utmost pandiculation
in the pursuit of Blue Squares,
attracted by their sides and colouring.

She was found bled white,
unhinged at three corners,
hiding in quadrate quandary,
by her elliptical home help.
Lost two whole sides she did,

and the blueness of youth.
Now only a hypotenuse graft
heals the gap, a 'one-line prayer'
free from the Red Cross
in the absence of Social Services
for squares in cylindrical caves.

Meanwhile ....

on the mountain top, seemingly,
an auto-cannibalistic hexagon
writhes in the geometrical throes
of unaccustomed self-absorption
– four sides green and crocodile-mouthed,
picnicking on two jointed ribs
swimming in blue fat topped
with a flotsam of jelly babies.

HORSE TREK
(to boldly come from where no horse ever came before)

The horse shot up from the earth
on hind legs in the fifth position
like a buck kangaroo in asbestos
travelling from the molten core.

It had emerged to celebrate the birthday
of Gloria Swanson
having tracked her DNA from first beginnings
in fossilised palaeozoic seaweed.

but its rider had lost his sense of time,
which was measured below the crust
by the revolving eyes of a sulphurous deity
with a passion for volcanoes.

FLIES TAKE NO UMBRAGE

Flies take no umbrage
at intent to murder
but quit the stage

appearing without malice
elsewhere, always alert
on another surface

contemptuous, brazen,
while the wall-slapping paper
of the slow-footed alien

smoking a white stalk
continues to miss,
amid coarse human talk

disturbing the air waves,
unable to hit them
(even on architraves).

This might be thought fit
reason for umbrage
but they do not take it.

Part 2

Survey and Bibliography

A SURVEY
OF THE WORK OF ERIC RATCLIFFE

Brian Louis Pearce

Eric Hallam Ratcliffe, one of the most original poets of his generation, was born at Teddington, Middlesex, on the 8th August 1918, under the sign of Leo. His father was a dentist, who at one time had his practice at 7 The Green, Twickenham. His nearness to the river and green places such as Bushy and Richmond Parks and Kew Gardens was to contribute to his deep rooted empathy with Nature and all things in it, together with his love of the sun and the inspiration he received from it, whilst the opportunity to roam or pause amid such untrammelled precincts fed that reflective spirit which must early have been latent in him. His lyrical *The Chronicle of the Green Man* (1960) was much of it written in Bushy Park he said. He was educated at Richmond Hill School; Kingston Grammar School, where he matriculated; and at Birkbeck College (London University) where he gained intermediate B.Sc. before his career was interrupted by the Second World War. Already the scientific bent of his mind had made itself felt, however, not only in his studies but in his joining the National Physical Laboratory (based then, as now at Teddington, bordering Bushy Park) as an Assistant Experimental Officer in the Metrology Division. He was 'called up' in 1938, as part of the 1st Militia, in the pre-war crisis at the time of 'Munich.' Posted to Aldershot as a private in the RAOC, he worked briefly as an instrument mechanic before volunteering for training as an ammunition examiner. Soon he was promoted to lance-corporal as part of a small team inspecting anti–aircraft ammunition and gun sites in the London area, including the location and destruction of unexploded shells in the Blitz. It was now that to his reflective and scientific nature was to be added the experience of India during what were still very formative years. In 1941 he was promoted to sergeant and posted to Bombay, and after a short posting to Ferozepore, found himself on the North-West Frontier i/c. ammunition during the Waziristan tribal operations of 1941/2. Promoted to warrant officer class 1, he lectured later on map reading, took PT classes and assisted training officers at Secunderabad; was in charge of an ammunition examination and repair team at Whitefields, finding opportunity to visit Mysore and Seringapatam (seeing Hyder Ali's tomb) when on leave. Returned to the UK he was posted to Shropshire, Leicester and Ascot, from which last station he was demobbed. This exposure to Indian thought is pervasive in its influence, but is caught in undisguised form in the short poem 'Ashram' in *Leo Poems* (1972):

> Thought was almost a wave-form,
> an elusive violet
> beamed from internal antennae;
> western truths were without substance.
>
> It was the way of non-violence;
> the spirit was on their faces,
>
> sun in their empty shoes,
> the spinning wheel ... a symbol.

In 1945 he returned to the National Physical Laboratory as an Assistant Experimental Officer in the Physics Division. He transferred to the Heat section, toward the end of the 1940s, and was to publish ten papers on thermal conductivity between 1957 and 1968. Years later, his work on glass was still being cited in the *Handbook of Chemistry and Physics* (Chemical Rubber Company, USA), a major reference tool for scientific data, enough recognition (and 'justification') one might think, for a life's work. Eventually his section was reduced to make way for atomic and molecular research and he took up a post at the Water Pollution

Laboratory, Stevenage, where he worked on *Water Pollution Abstracts* and edited for the press various papers on water pollution. He already held a translator's certificate for scientific Russian, and by the late sixties had acquired a number of other qualifications from evening classes, including Technical Authorship and Membership of the Institute of Information Scientists.. He was then 52, yet from that day to this there has been no cessation of his projections of visionary schemes for thesauruses, periodical listings, biographies, and experimental forms of chess, an amazing number of which took life and shape. He closed his official career with early retirement at 56 as Senior Experimental Officer, but then took up a full-time appointment with the Institute of Electrical Engineers, editing electrical journals until he was 60, when the rules compelled him to 'retire'. He then diverted himself by obtaining a 'B' licence as a ham radio operator.

Yet all this scientific and peripherally inventive work, for which he can take great credit, was as nothing to him, one would imagine, compared with his literary work. It is unquestionably in that field that his most fecund and original talents manifest themselves, related as they are to his deep interest in pre-Roman history, and his philosophical and religious concerns, whilst utilising, too, his gift for conceptual invention, and linguistic facility with word, image and phrase. Indeed, his strength (and occasional difficulty) as a poet lies in his gift for imagery, which he exercises, arguably, at the expense of more obvious, traditional lyric structures and patterns of jingly sound. Yet he has his own phrasing and sound-loveliness, as one comes to know his work, which achieves a permanent effect in the mind of any sympathetic reader, creating its own quite individual world. It is amazing that he has written so much poetry, and that he has done so whilst engaged in so much editorial work - of which his work with *Ore* (commenced 1954) is only one example - and whilst carrying on his scientific work for the whole of a normal working life's span. It is impressive for its range and volume, for the sheer creative urge and achievement it represents, as well as for its extreme originality in content and style. He is not without a puckish humour, too, which shines through a great deal of his work - and correspondence - as well as

B-5

in his so-called lighter verse such as *The Infidelium*, 1989, but above all he is driven by his daemon. He is a poet of the Muse, the muse of the green earth, the muse of woman and fecundity, and the muse of poetry and the artistic process and impetus itself. Early in the 1960s he joined the Druid Order and in 1965 commenced a short-lived journal *The Druid*, editing its last issue while on special leave at the British Library at Wetherby to gain experience for the move from bench science to information work.

He married in 1947, divorced in 1969. His daughter Sheila Ann, born in 1949, sadly died in 1983. Cf. his publication *Sheila Ann Ratcliffe 1949-83* (with Vanessa Kemberey), Ore, 1984. Illustrative of his stamina and excess, almost, of diverse physical and intellectual powers, in 1966, the year he was 48, he finished in the first half of a marathon from Windsor to St Albans in aid of the Abbey Theatre. He has suffered innumerable setbacks, but surmounted or, at worst, endured them all, with the impeccable good humour of the man who could write: "I am living in a shed, at the bottom of a garden, applying my knowledge of thermal conductivity and insulation in order to keep warm."

It involved newspapers, I believe.

On another occasion, likewise in the late 1960s, he explained: "Having grown a beard, I am now completely unrecognisable. I have been provided with a comfortable room, telephone, carpet, and coffee brought to the door per trolley. Down below the sewage experts are negotiating their unaesthetic experimentations and it is just a case of praying that the wind blows in the right direction."

His preferences in music circa 1970 were then Sibelius, Wagner and Grieg. He liked Graves' prose, not his poetry, and Henry Treece's novels, and also responded to John Cowper Powys, some letters of whose he once published (Ore, 1971), and of whom he wrote:

I think that what attracts me so much to J.C. Powys' work is his feeling for legend and myth, and his philosophy of absorption in atmosphere; to lose one's ego-centricity in the comings and goings of imaginative processes.

In poetry he has confessed to having been influenced by Dylan and Edward Thomas, "bits of Kipling", "some of Masefield and De la Mare"; Yeats. He owns to a special 'fondness' for Chesterton's 'Ballad of the White Horse' and for the poems of the old Welsh bards in translation. There is affinity, I think, with the younger writer Peter Redgrove who shares his fecundity, his resource of original imagery, his scientific training and his feeling for the material and psychic world and for the intermingling of each, distinct as the two writers are. In 1981 (Interim Press), Ratcliffe contributed an essay to an edition of David Jones' 'The Narrows' and indeed, one would assume Jones to be a writer with whom he would have affinity, if only at the overlap between Jones' Roman and Ratcliffe's (by and large) pre-Roman world. His middle name of Hallam stems from his maternal grandfather who was an occasional companion of W.E. Henley (on whom Ratcliffe has written), but neither Henley, nor Tennyson for that matter, have had much influence on his own (poetic) work.

He was contributing verse to the *RAOC Gazette* whilst in India, but it was not until 1952 that his first publication appeared. This was *The Visitation*, a poem of some 250 lines, published when he was 34. It is the poet's 'Intimations of Immortality', and indeed it quotes Wordsworth's poem in an epigraph. There may be doubt as to whether the poem succeeds as a whole – the aspirant poet is not always in full control of his imagery and structure, arguably – yet it contains many passages of permanent beauty and validity, and its omission from *Fire in the Bush : poems 1955-1992*, Salzburg University, 1993 (hereinafter referred to as *FITB*) is one of my few regrets about that excellent book, a comprehensive, long-overdue and well-planned, accessible anthology of Ratcliffe's best work, to which these present comments make, I hope, a useful introduction or complement. *The Visitation* is intriguing, not only for its many fine passages, thoughts and images, but for the insight it gives into the poet's style in formation. It contains an indictment of modern civilised man (c.pp.13-14) and a celebration of the primordial, 'maternal', perennially vernal, creation. The very variety of subject, mood and style subsumed beneath the larger intention is itself impressive and produces passages both evocatively accessible:

> Leviathans, Atlantic pounding,
> Rising and slow sinking steel,
> Prow–heaving in wide winter seas
> Toward invisible horizons
> Shrouded in wet velvet bitterness　　　　　　(*V* :7)

and related to his own experience up to the time of composition, as
in these lines of equally sharp impact and realism:

> Shells, gloss painted yellow, black and green
> Batched and sub–batched, quiet in brown boxes
> Until the System shouts and splinters steel
> Which strikes blood blossoms on the lip of truth.　　(*V* :9)

It would be interesting to know whether he composed the draft of
the poem in one sitting, circa the date of publication, or whether it
was not an integration of passages written earlier, at diverse times
and places, in India, on a troopship, in the English countryside, in
a parlour or by the seacoast, and brought together in a single text
much as Eliot might have managed it, though the effect and style is
naturally different. The essence of his appeal lies in his thought,
which was to develop into the fascination of a work such as the
recent large-scale *The Experiment* (*FITB* :136-173) and,
particularly at this early period, perhaps, his sensitive and delicate
response to Nature; the observation and careful, evocative phrases
with which he describes it:

> Autumn in England;
> Red sun over the counties, resolute, glowing;
> Country lattice panes crystalled in dusk walls;
> Gloom–worn,gentle–leaved gardens;elf moss on old eaves;
> Gipsy winds in the pine scent, scattering, blowing.
> Later only the snow, fields' dereliction,
> and hedge–line loneliness veined on earth's white hands.
> 　　　　　　　　　　　　　　　　　(*V* :11)

The subtle and varied rhythms of the lines, and that careful phrasing, are behind their modest-seeming appeal. It is as though the poet, like Nature itself, will not often speak out. His effect, like Nature's, is achieved gradually and undemonstratively. He is content to be true. And is it not this very reticence - his refusal to seek immediate effect or applause, sufficiently and all-absorbed as he is in the creative task - which promises for his work part of its permanent value and appeal? That other-worldliness which is founded in, and so appreciative of, the sensuous here and now? Notice the mellow 'l' sounds and the alliterative 'n's used instinctively, with an early mastery, in the Shakespearian (or Dylan Thomas-esque?) utterance:

> Hoarsely into the quiet nun night
> She cried oblivion. (*V* :13)

- which instigates a mood of negation, and that indictment of mankind we have mentioned, culminating in the bare desolation of:

> Now they are gone,
> May God preserve the peace of an empty world (*V* :14)

But negation is not the final or only word. It rarely is with Ratcliffe. For one thing there is the way in which archetypal images, lodged by time in the human spirit, are utilised and transformed - and found, as throughout his work, to retain their power to move the (ostensibly modern?) mind. Take this folk-echoing rhymed passage, which serves for interlude:

> All, all must go, clad in moth yellow
> Who slew the elm, slew the ash, slew the cat-willow.
> Scorned they the apple breath, ghosts of the tunes,
> Violet blossoms, marigold noons. (*V* :13)

- 'green' thirty years before the present movement and in a deeper sense. For another thing there is the coda of this poem - only nine lines, but lines that leave us assured that beauty and creative life are meant to triumph over every apparent negation:

> The tide took.
>
> White moon on razor rock,
> Stale dew,
> The green shock of ghost seas
> And the ring and the ring and the ring
> Of the small beach stones –
> Only wind dragging the brake,
> And the wild witch call of the young moon.
>
> The flower had returned.   (*V* :14)

Little Pagan (1955) was published by Bill Turner who contributes the Foreword to *Fire in the Bush*. There are hints of Dylan Thomas, as in 'The Suicides' and 'The Ragnarök Rocket Bomb' but they grow fainter, as his work proceeds and are, even here, submerged in his own quite distinct mood and style which we would immediately recognise as 'Ratcliffian'. There is a touch of Tolkien, too, when we have entered:

> the shimmering land of whispers
> and watched the wraiths divide ...
>
>   (*FITB* :18 'The Throw')

or seen:

> boys and girls, armies and ghosts
> who move as threads through his blue mountains ...
>
>   (*FITB* :17 'The Green Man')

In the beautiful 'The White River' (*Anthropos* & *FITB*) he describes in his own archetypal terms the moment of finding an empathic companion. The shaking boy discovers:

> a playmate from the avenue of flowers
> calling quietly along the white river
> his forgotten name   (*FITB* :14)

It is the theme of Kipling's 'Brushwood Boy' and of Hofmannsthal and Strauss's *Arabella*, and of lyric poets from time immemorial, yet Ratcliffe handles it in his own refined, very personal way. The outstanding poem in this pamphlet, however, is surely 'Death was no Empty Hat' (*Anthropos & FITB*), unique in statement and form. The poem is set out in a sonnet's octet and sestet but, while intrinsically lyrical, has not a sonnet's line-length or rhyme-scheme. The basic scheme is one of a five-stressed line followed by one of three, and the poem vividly, marvellously implies that death is not something final or dreadful, but a swinging upward, as on a trapeze, with all its grace and elegance, to a richer and fuller life:

> ... a swung trapeze
> swept through a hall of song.
> Hung on a silver wire, the winging bar
> leaped ...   (*FITB* :21)

Another *Little Pagan* poem, 'Nuclear Heritage' - like 'Cyclic Adam' with its 'Last Man' - prefigures the magnificent *The Ragnarök Rocket Bomb* (*FITB* :23-25) published in October 1957. It is understandable that poets of the initial atom-bomb era, post 1945, should be preoccupied with its grim and cataclysmic implications. It is a cause for concern, indeed, if the fifty years that have ensued have dimmed our apprehension of it. Edith Sitwell's poems on the subject are well known. Ratcliffe's, too, have telling validity. 'Nuclear Heritage' (*FITB* :19) is set out in 6-line stanzas, with the third and sixth lines rhyming, sometimes 'thorn/dawn', sometimes 'cauldron/children' as Ian Caws might do it, with a firm 3-stressed line. *The Ragnarök Rocket Bomb* (*FITB* : 23-25) has its affinities with Dylan Thomas and Edith Sitwell, and his familiar Celtic and Arthurian imagery. But it is notable above all for its sustained force and impetus; the thrust which shapes its overall achievement. The opening passage can be read as having three stresses to the line, though there is subtlety and variety within this scheme, and at the heart of the poem a 4-stressed pattern predominates. It is the vigour of the concern – that spirit of lament and prophecy that becomes paean – that enthuses its verbal and rhythmic vigour: that feeling for what may pass that becomes in the seer's hands something akin to celebration. Here he is, indeed, one with the old Welsh bards, the Old Testament prophets and the *scop* or *makar* of the Battle of Maldon, yet absolutely of his generation and utterly himself, as he deals with this nuclear reality that no poets before his day could know. The outline of the bomb's effect can be traced in a long and magnificent passage (some 38 lines) of a hard lyric intensity:

> It has broken the bones of buried playmates ...
> It has broken the old breasts of boulders ...
> It has crushed the stone anchors of dead men ...
> It has killed the rolling hound bells ...   (*FITB* :23-24)

We are left with

> ... a god's tear
> which fell, and found no root to cherish.   (*FITB* :25)

The *Transitions* pamphlet of 1957 contained six poems. 'Death was no Empty Hat' is reprinted in it. 'The Suicides' (*FITB* : 27) is a strong poem in four stanzas. "Shining in the good queen summer" (first line) it conjures for one reader the poet of "I see the boys of summer in their ruin" or '"And Death shall have no Dominion." 'Old Fragrance' (*FITB* :30 & *Anthropos*) and 'Century House' (*FITB* :29 & *Anthropos*) are two pieces of gentle nostalgia. The rough good humour of 'The Celestial Landlady' is omitted from *FITB*. It has affinities with 'Nurse, Teddington Hospital' and 'Flower Girl, Isleworth Hospital', both in *Leo Poems* (1972) (*FITB* 73 & 74):

> Yet someone had given her glen talk,
> taught her to enclose a sweetness in the husk of words;

to be an artiste before stroke-seared old men
until they felt within their map of bones
the keen warmth of a summer to come,
and knew for a chalice the small glass in their hands.

(FITB :73)

or

She is a tawny thruster, this Eliza.

(FITB :74)

No lack of humanity, or of accessibility, there. Surely these deserve to be recognised as anthology pieces in the most complimentary sense. Their authorship is unmistakeable, yet their appeal is to everyone, surely, and they speak from the heart to the heart. 'Sestina to a Friend' (*Leo Poems* : *FITB* :76/7), like 'God and Mammon' in the *Leo Mysticus* publication of 1989 (published when he was 70), also in sestina form (cf *FITB* :133/4) illustrates his command of traditional forms, when he chooses to use them, though his imagery and ethos remain absolutely his own. Such an example brings to mind how much of Ratcliffe's oeuvre has been published since he reached his 'allotted span', culminating (to date) in 'The Experiment' sequence to which we shall return. Lyrically, however, it is arguable that Ratcliffe is at his best in his forties, in a poem like 'Listening Boy' (*Transitions* : *FITB* :28):

I was a giant who plied the free bold hills,
with the heel of a hickory tree and a toy of iron,
and strode five leagues in boots of elephant hide,
when Jill was alive, and I her listening boy.
. . .
I was the man who grieved to watch his friend
yield her temple warmth to the mask of evening,
when she died, as the sun fades on a barley field,
with no word for her listening boy.

and, consummately in *Mist on my Eyes* (1961) which I have written about at length in *The Art of Eric Ratcliffe* (1970) and still regard

B-13

as an outstanding book. In it his twin preoccupations of pre-AD 400 history and woman as Muse both find themselves, it seems to me, in lyric utterance of great distinction and originality. In poems like 'Roman Silchester' (*FITB* :48), 'Forever' (*FITB* :52-53), and 'The Passing of the Tribe' (*FITB* :66) the first-named theme is developed, while in 'Mary and the Millwater Bells' (*FITB* :50-51) the 'Muse' is apotheosised triumphantly in lines of subtle enveloping length:

Then on the air-stirred earth, you were the movement of all beautiful women / the maple cheery girl – the traveller under the head-dress of the south wind.

In the shorter pieces 'Stolen Property' (*FITB* :54), 'The Gentle Raider' (*FITB* :55), 'The Maiden of the Moon's Boat' (*Anthropos & FITB* :57), 'A Lady Kneeling for Holy Communion' (*FITB* :59), and 'Slave Girl' (*FITB* :60) the idea of woman as Muse is further explored; in several of these poems, in conjunction with the historical preoccupation and setting. Thus we have the Viking who "crouched once" in 'The Gentle Raider.' Among the finest poems in this collection (and his whole oeuvre), however, are several which partake only marginally of these twin themes. In 'The Northland Men' (*FITB* :64) for example, the mood echoes Arnold's 'Forsaken Merman' while the free but subtle internal rhyming (men/caves; men/waves; night/light; sea/we is worth studying for its own sake. 'The Unnecessary Silence' (*FITB* :65) incorporates the nuclear concern in lines at once grave and flowing. 'Elegy for my Uncle buried at Girton' (*FITB* :63) has the lyric immediacy of 'Listening Boy' and is a taut-rhymed poem in ABABA form:

When priors of space and time advance their crosses
to long white men who crystallise their flesh,
what hills, what singing earths collect the losses
of those who see their friends pass through the mesh
of green and silence underneath the mosses?

'Lines for Any Dead Poet' (*FITB* :61) is not so much a lament as a description of the poetic impulse and temperament, and of the poet's oneness with the world of Nature:

> All his, once, the wind's rock, the tripod lock of roots,
> the petal whimper, the starting sap and swept impulse,
> the tiny triggered senses.

Subsequent poems that combine the woman as Muse idea, with his delicate, highly individual spirituality (a universal and ecumenical sprituality for the most part) are the beautiful 'On Light' (*Leo Poems : FITB* :72) and 'Parallel Travellers' (*Leo Poems : FITB* :68). 'Corpse' (*Anthropos & FITB* :129) and 'Ages unto Ages' (*FITB* :124) echo themes of *Mist on my Eyes* with which Seamus Heaney is familiar, while poems with titles like 'Elaine', 'Thea', 'Jean', 'The Observer on the Train','Eucia ...', 'Rosamund' find the feminine 'Muse' predominant. Of lyric poems I have left for last mention the brilliant season exposition 'Herb and Hooligan' (*FITB* :85) :

> Once briefly were petals divided and sprung
> ...
> the witches stole, with lanterns of gold
> ...
> like a mad doctor probing, Winter pushed
> thumbs in the keen dried lattice leaves ...

- and 'The Spirit of the Green Light' (*A Sun-Red Mantle & FITB* :114) :

> With your green light held high, raise
> your maid–arm pointed,
> sing against blood–letting, be of love
> like those who drew water
> ...
> Soft witch, abide and sing
> of Moses, Molmutius and Hu Gadarn,
> of Ezra, Howel, and Yesu,
> dispensers of white glory ...

- in which the poet's hospitality of spirit is plain. It is a key poem in making its affirmation of the poet's spirituality, and in demonstrating that this poet who has studied science and been involved in war – who has been "kept very busy in detecting and helping to make safe our own unexploded anti-aircraft shells, which often returned to earth with failed primitive and damp gunpowder fuses" – and has suffered many sadnesses and reverses, can retain deepset at the root and heart of his poetry, as in his everyday demeanour, the spirit of love and gentleness and of irrepressible good humour and hope. His conscious spirituality is a a compound of many inputs; ancient and modern, western and eastern, Christian, Jewish, Druid, Indian and theosophical. Concepts of acausalism, syncretism, telepathic parallelism, combine with what one might call the race-image granary, and the Qabalistic Tree of Life to find their point of rest (or fusion) in a finally patterned product of a deeply read and pondered mind, at once poetic, religious and scientific, that can as yet out-compute computers in the poet's particular associative-cum-constructive process. And bring to dark places light. For conscious as he is of matter and the primordial;

cf. 'The Coming of the Tribe' (*FITB* :47)

primitive existence;

cf. 'The Hunter', 'Eucia the Briton Greets the Dawn' (*FITB* :118-119)

war, havoc and catastrophe;

cf. 'Nuclear Heritage' (*FITB* :19), 'The Ragnarök Rocket Bomb' (*FITB* : 23-25), 'The Unnecessary Silence' (*FITB* :65)

loss:

cf. 'The Listening Boy' (*FITB* :28,), 'Elegy for my Uncle' (*FITB* :63); and can evoke them so finely, he sees the inner and final meaning of all things as soul-consciousness, with spiritual devotion and fulfilment as the 'jewel in the crown', the consummate empathy of poetry and life alike;

cf. 'A Lady Kneeling for Holy Communion' (*FITB* :59), 'On Light' (*FITB* :72), 'Ashram' (*FITB* :83), and 'The Spirit of the Green Light' (*FITB* :114).

It is the same with the longer poems. We have seen that his 1952 long poem *The Visitation* ended with an affirmative note after its evocation of "winter seas", the "seated crone", and shells, "gloss-painted."

The dramatic lyric *The Chronicle of the Green Man* (1960; 1977; *FITB* :31-45) explores the symbolic and unknown "by the light of sense knowledge, or that which underlies the conscious activities of the brain." It ends with "lovers with temple hands holding the Everlasting Man" and with a word picture of Samuel Palmer's Nature-rooted visionary painting 'Coming from Evening Church.'

Warrior of the Icenian Queen (1973) relates in 3-lined verses the thoughts and feelings of an Icenian warrior who served in the AD 60 Boudiccan revolt, and includes italic passages of ghost voices. Rosemary Sutcliff in her appreciative foreword describes it as reading "uncannily like the real thing."

> I heard the cries, I remember,
> putting sticks on the fire one rainy night
> and kicking the ashes   (*FITB* :87-100 (88))

The related piece *Commius* (Quarto Press, 1976, handset in hammer uncial and lectura by John B. Easson in an edition of 325 copies) uses the same stanza to evoke a charismatic cavalry leader associated with the Gallic Vercingetorix's revolt, and with varied exploits in Britain and on the Continent, culminating in his establishment as a tribal king at Calleva (Silchester) circa the middle years of the first century AD, during which time he issued coins with 3-tailed mare patterns and arguably was the husband of Kreidyla (the Cordelia of King Lear). Ratcliffe contributes explanatory prefaces to the original text (p.5) and to *FITB* :101-112 (101). He also published 'Notes to Commius' from *Ore* at the time of the appearance of the first edition. Here are those "dormant stored items" he speaks of which, once part of the individual or race experience, are recovered by "an association mechanism switched on by ... events involving the poet":

> and the fingers of warriors were firm
> in the first light; like midnight horses

their hair streamed in the wind; ...

But I had a vision to put aside,
swung in the darkness of the sleeping night
– a black flower and grasses,

towering clouds and landstorms,
sheetheads of sky axes,
a bird–high wailing

and a moon forest singing with dead men's bells,
my comrades with phantom spears
remote as water–branches,

and our sea routes blocked with dream galleys
launched from curving ghost harbours
in pale green waters.

After three sunsets we came to Bibrax
– a frowning circle of high–beaked walls
– a camp of dark traitors

peeping like mongrels through rampart gaps
– jack–faced, small crouching townsmen
whose minds were Caesar's ...   (*FITB* : 107–108)

The seven parts of *The Experiment* 1991-2 (*FITB* :136-173) are a
late attempt at synthesis of pre-history (*Advent*), war, (*Hill 60*),
nationhood (*Components of the Nation*), science, and a belief in an
after-life, the deepening spiritual consciousness of the incarnated
soul (*Scientary* ; *Ghosts of the Quaternary* ; *Ark*). The attempt
meets with remarkable success, and by its post-Bunting, post-Eliot
integration of many different themes and styles reminds us how a
long poem may be written in an age of so much disintegration and
transition.

> What early child-forms moved the moments
> near flower scent, in sunlight or in shadow,
> or in the wind-high grasses ...
> -a leaf-faith fading in the crocus memory?
>
> (*Advent* & *FITB* :138)

Hill 60 is the point of entry, I think, with its narrative elements from varied periods and places, but with an emphasis on the 1st World War. Part V (*FITB* :151-152) is a fine passage, evoking the tragedy and waste by attention to detail, focusing close up, before panning again for a wider view:

> What of the lock of golden hair
> curled in the tunic of the pilot Hun –
> and why should the flyer cherish that one,
> yet kill the other in an accident of death? ...
>
> Here lay the embryos grown from the 1890s
> whose mothers graced days at Chantilly ...

– while the concluding part VI brings it all together in 3-lined stanzas of lyric clarity:

> Does the arrow-pull muscle now push a death-button?
>
> (153)

'Ghosts of the Quaternary' gives us:

> Pale wafers on the mind-tree,
> unborn phantoms pulse to birth ...   (163)

whilst the passage commencing "Where are the bones of Morfa Rhiannedd" (V, 166) with its thrusting juxtapositions of proper names from different epochs, its conjunction of idioms, conjures David Jones' *In Parenthesis* and *The Anathemata*, as does the military understratum of 'Hill 60'. Section II of 'Ark' is a beautiful passage that concludes in the arms of psalms, 'l's and 'm's:

B-19

In time's gallow seas
the fish swim shallow,
silt piles, envelopes
a million Edens;
a thimble of faith,
a pittance of psalms
lost in eternity,
a Saviour's arms
historicity.   (*FITB* :170)

"Poverty of historicism" (Popper's phrase) or not, this is poetry that lures one on to read it (and to *think*) surely, and 'The Experiment' seems a fitting consummation of his work to date.

The lighter verse to be found in *Anthropos* (cf. the section 'The Flip Side') needs less commentary. It is significant that he has produced this puckish contemporary work throughout his career, cf. *Ballet Class* (1986), many of the poems in which were written much earlier. One of its best 'My Celestial Landlady' was in *Transitions* (1957). This is a-typical and not really 'light' verse in my opinion, but has his more archetypal poetry's originality and verve. In 'The Experiment', too, there are signs of the two genres getting closer, and that is another direction he might take.

He seems to have published more 'light' work in recent years, cf. *The Ballad of Polly McPoo* (1991) and *The Man in Green Combs* (1993). A good deal of his work in the genre relates to woman as Muse, and simply shows a different approach to one of his (and the race's!) abiding subjects. *The Infidelium* (1989), his long poem in 4-lined stanzas rhyming ABBA like Tennyson's *In Memoriam*, has an 18th century feel to it, and is perhaps his most sustained 'lighter' achievement. Asked to provide an epigraph for it, the present writer essayed:

True son of Twickenham, or Teddington,
our hero writes like Whitehead, Cambridge, Pope,
catches at heartstrings like a tar a rope,
jests like Fitzgerald, boxed 'twixt drains and sun.

Anthropos is remarkable on its own terms, quite apart from the fact that it comes from a writer entering upon his seventy-seventh year. In it we find him taking that new turn presaged by *The Experiment*, integrating time and mood. The Salzburg University Press is indeed to be congratulated on drawing this further collection of work out into the open: work, that is, for the most part extremely 'accessible'; a good deal of it recently written and little known, and much of it contriving with virile invention to merge contemporary experience with the primordial-cum-Roman scene. The opening section Historical Flesh is very strong with a fine poem 'Small Sarah' that has affinities with *Mist on My Eyes* and some of the longer poems. Its 'mother/protector' images in part III of the poem, hark back to *The Visitation* in mood, and give new expression to something he has always handled well:

> race pillar, rain shielder of small ones,
> protector from the rodded lightning,
> soother of the ills of venture fields,
> ... you were the shaped window
> opened for sunlight ...   (*A*:9)

'Caractacus in Oxford Street' is well observed and links past and present with its "small rushing wheels/carrying the uncloaked in metal chariots." The 'accessibility' of this work derives I think from the heightened 'narrative-intensity' of what we might call its narrative lyrics. 'Vedica' with her body "like a book, carefully loaned", is particularly good. The occasional use of Roman technical or jargon words here, as elsewhere, is an echo of David Jones that I find works. 'The Dream Catcher' and 'The Integration' will repay study, though not all this sort of thing finds a sufficiently specific or lay-friendly correlation in which its abstractions may have focus. However, in '*Experimenta Lucifera* ' which follows them there is a new kind of material, "light along the rubrics ... flowing the Word to the reaching heart ... skill engaging with scroll and line,/close-holding energy in patterns/ultimate in Celtic purity and tone." (*A*:44). In 'The Overwalking' there are references to 'Hill 60'; and signs of an acknowledged influence in the title 'And Life

B-21

Shall Have no Dominion.' Some shorter lines in 'The Overwalking' are very effective, whilst in a poem on Barts priory church in London there is fine (and for Ratcliffe) rare use of a changing refrain: "*Sancte Bartholemeo Ora Pro Nobis.* " (*A*:60). 'Geomantic Love' (*A*:67) is small, Chinese-evocative and lovely. 'Amulets' (*A*:71) is again different in its use of couplets; yet the poem has the intrinsic Ratcliffian feel. The world of 'Small Sarah' is called up again in 'The Cave' (*A* :69). The mood of the poet is summed, I think, in 'Inside *Thalassus Marinus*, (*A* :72-73) where, "poet of immediate terrors" who has had strange mistresses", he speaks of "incompleteness" and ends (erroneously in this reader's opinion): "I am not yet made." In that spirit-fed confession, and the communion of present and past, lies the nub of the book.

His editorial and entrepreneurial work has been various, if sometimes short-lived. He is a man of ideas, constantly conjuring new projects. Yet his patient and generous work as editor of *Ore* has been continued for over 40 years (including a gap of several years after issue 10), so that as I write the magazine nears its 50th and probably last issue. He has written essays and biography and founded poetry groups, e.g. the Richmond Poetry Group, starting as the Whitton group in the early sixties and continuing until 1984, when it merged with the Richmond Writers Circle. He has been hospitable, too, in his use of the *Ore* imprint for many an aspirant or recognised writer, and has encouraged poets, over the years, both in their formative and their subsequent stages. He has been a scientist and a soldier, and done his share of dangerous war-work, as we have seen, yet it is as the poet of *Fire in the Bush* and as that rare thing, an unassuming, kindly charismatical figure, that he seems likely to endure when nobody who has met him is left. The writer recalls him presiding over his Teddington young poets' prizegiving, that blossomed into a Richmond competition which still continues; passing at rapid speed (signally out of keeping with his age and appearance) on his way to work at the NPL; lighting a joss stick; peering at a poem or an Indian meal as though it was an unexploded bomb; explaining to the police why strange people had come to his flat to read poems and not to smoke pot, depositing only normal cigarette ash in the trays provided; speaking about the

Tree of Life to an engrossed audience of three; processing in druid ceremonial, as swordbearer; a man who should have been a 'keeper of the dead', whether at Richmond, Avebury or the Kennet Longbarrows; the man in his dressing gown at Charing Cross hospital grinning as he chatted away happily, his head full of new ideas; my fellow-guest (reader) at Tunbridge Wells, as we stood for a few minutes, exchanging reminiscences outside the arts centre, our feet on uneven red slabs; the outstanding, inspired, truly-bardic poet of his generation, of whom I wrote, when I thought he was vanishing from us:

Old Wise Man

No wiser or kinder,
less self-concerned jester,
than he, the dear fellow,
have I ever known. Wish
I were there with him, were
he where I could guest a
night's talk. Night will blow o-
ver us all but he'll fish

for wisdom in his box
high in the lonely tower,
bent over his books. If
bombs fell he would go on
baiting thoughts as though stocks
of time were his. The power
of his brave rod looks stiff
but could defuse London

now as in the Blitz. More
like Plato's oddfellow
than most I've known, and so
gentle with it, he's played
the part of guide to scores
of awed parties, elbow-

ing obstacles, let time go
for a walk, while he made

truth over tea. If he's
gone on a journey, we
are the poorer without
him. Is there no sighting
of a bearded and wheez–
y old wise man, rheumy,
twinkling rapport? Pop out
and hear if he's talking

The Frogmore Papers
City Whiskers

_____ oOo _____

BIBLIOGRAPHY

BIOGRAPHY

Sheila Ann Ratcliffe 1949–1983 (with Vanessa Kemberey). Ore,1984; *The Golden Heart Man.* Astrapost, 1993; *William Ernest Henley (1849–1903) an Introduction.* Astrapost,1993 (also see Special Issue of *Ore* (No.28) on Henley); *The Caxton of Her Age: the career and family background of Emily Faithfull.* Images, 1993.

HISTORY, LEGEND

The Great Arthurian Timeslip. Ore, 1978; *The French King: Commius and the legend of Lear.* Astrapost, 1990; *Winstanley's Walton, 1649. Events in the Civil War at Walton–on–Thames.* Astrapost, 1994.

POETRY   (LV = light verse)

The Visitation. Stockwell, 1952; *Litttle Pagan.* The Poet, 1955; *The Ragnarök Rocket–Bomb.* Guild Press, 1957; *Transitions.* Linden Press, 1957; *The Chronicle of the Green Man.* Ore, 1960 and 1977; *Mist on my Eyes.* Guild Press, 1961; *Leo Poems.* Ore, 1973; *Warrior of the Icenian Queen.* Ore, 1973; *Commius.* Quarto Press, 1976; *A Sun–Red Mantle.* Mitre Press, 1976; *Nightguard of the Quaternary.* Outposts, 1979; *Ballet Class.* Ore, 1986. LV; *Leo Mysticus.* Astrapost, 1989; *The Infidelium.* Astrapost, 1989. LV; *The Runner of the Seven Valleys.* Astrapost, 1990; *The Ballad of Polly McPoo.* Astrapost, 1991. LV.

THE EXPERIMENT : *Kingdoms* (Astrapost, 1991); *Hill 60* (Astrapost, 1991); *Scientary* (Astrapost, 1991); *Ghosts of the Quaternary* (Astrapost, 1992); *Components of the Nation* (Astrapost, 1992); *Ark* (Diamond Press, 1992); *Advent* (Green Lantern Press, 1992).

The Man in Green Combs. Astrapost, 1993. LV; *Fire in the Bush : Poems 1955–1992.* Univ. of Salzburg, 1993.

ARTICLES, ESSAYS

Gleanings for a Daughter of Aeolus : essays and poetry for Alcyone. Stevenage (author), 1968, 13pp; The 'Narrows' and the Western Empire. In *The Narrows : David Jones.* Budleigh Salterton, Interim Press, 1981; Helen of Essex, empress and saint. *Essex Countryside,* Nov. 1982, 36–38 and (abridged) *Pendragon,* 1983, **XVI**, 3, 6–8 ; Commius : the background. *New Celtic Review,* Feb.–Apr. 1984, 12–15; Poetic activity and consciousness. *Acumen,* 1988, No.7, 39–42; Poetry as a survival factor. *Creative New World,* 1988, **10**, 22–23; Romantic acausalism, Pts 1 & 2. *Creative New World,* 1989, **13**, 22– 25 and **14**, 18–21.

SCIENCE

Papers

The thermal conductivities of plastics. *Plastics,* 1957, **22**, 55; The thermal conductivities of fused and crystalline quartz. *J.appl.Phys.,* 1959, **10**, 22; The thermal conductivities of ocean sediments. *J.Geophys.Res.,* 1960, **65**, 1535; Preliminary measurements to determine the effect of composition on the thermal conductivity of glass. *Phys.Chem.Glasses,* 1960, **1**, 103; Thermal conductivity of silicone rubber and some other elastomers. *Trans. Inst. Rubber Inst.,* 1962, **38**, T181; The thermal conductivity of ice: new data on the temperature coefficient. *Phil.Mag.,* 1962, **7**, 1197; A survey of the most probable values for the thermal conductivities of glasses between about −150°C and 100°C, including new data on twenty–two glasses and a working formula for the calculation of conductivity from composition. *Glass Technol.,* 1963, **4**, 113; Wood: a review of data on thermal conductivity. *Wood,* 1964, Jul., Aug., Sept.; The thermal conductivities of plastics with glass, asbestos and cellulosic fibre reinforcement. *Appl.Mat.Res.,* 1966, 200; Estimation of the effective conductivities of two–phase media. *J.appl.Chem.,* 1968, **18**, 25; Automation in sewage works, sewerage systems, water supply and treatment, and the treatment of trade waste waters. An annotated bibliography. WPR Rep. 446R, Water Pollution Research Laboratory, Dept. of the Environment, March 1974, 40pp.

References in textbooks

Handbook of Chemistry and Physics. (U.S.A.) Annual. Tables of conductivities of glasses.

Conductivité Thermique : André Missenard (Edns Eyrolles,Paris, 1965). 15 refs.

Citations in scientific journals

These, by other authors, 1965–74 only (ref. *Citation Index*) are too numerous to quote in full, but they include papers by the following:

Becher, Beck, Boger, Bott, Bros, Budd, Cernak, Chaurasi, Chechelu, Cheng, Childs, Christof, Clulow, Combs, Corry, Costain, Damon, Davis, Decker, Devyatkova, Diment, Erickson, Fritz, Glanz, Glew, Gow, Hart, Hattori. Henyey, Herzen, Hutt, Hyndman, Johnson, Jongsma, Judge, Kassmeyer, Kasen, Klemens, Korgen, Lachenbruch, Langseth, Lewis, Likens, Lister, Lohe, Luscal, Lyobimov, Macdonald, Mizutani, Ozawa, Pitman, Popova, Puranen, Pye, Reiter, Robertson, Rosser, Sass, Schubert, Seidenst, Serruya, Smith, Suemone, Sugawara, Sundstrom, Swanberg, Van Velde, Vesselov, Von Herze, Walsh, Warren, Zeller.

PUBLISHING ACTIVITIES

Ore Nos 1–50, *The Druid* , Nos 1–2.

Ore Pubns (1969–1982): *The Chariot Poets* : No.1 Brian Louis Pearce; No.2 Ellen E.H. Collins; No.3 Eric Ratcliffe; No.4 Ithell Colquhoun; No.5 Frederic Vanson; No.6 Helen Shaw; No.7 Tony Rowe;No.8 Frederic Vanson; No.9 Olive Bentley; No.10 Helen Shaw. *Torches of the Island* : No.1 Ron Staley.

Ore Pubns (1971). *John Cowper Powys : Letters to Glyn Hughes,* edited by Dr. Bernard Jones, 24pp.

MISCELLANEOUS WORK

Notes on copyright, including references to the report of the Whitford Committee. *Aslib. Proc.,* 1979, 334; *Ratcliffe's Megathesaurus.* Hilltop Press, 1995.

Unpublished lyrics set to music and on tape include 'Boadicea Sue' (on Radio Bedford), 'Megalith Fair', 'Capricorn Girl', 'Lady of the Slalom', 'Black Lovely', 'Gypsy Trinket', Sitter–Bed Girl'.

Les Echecs Processionaires ou la Chenille. *Nouveaux Jeux D'Echecs Non Orthodoxes* .Joseph Boyer, Paris, 1954, p.86.

Brian Louis Pearce, poet and author, is an occasional lecturer at the National Portrait Gallery, London. His recent books include *Jack O' Lent, Leaving the Corner,* and *Thames Listener* (University of Salzburg) : poems 1949-89; *London Clay,* stories, *The Servant of his Country,* and other fiction. Cf. *Emotional Geology* : the writings of Brian Louis Pearce, Stride symposium, 1993.

The Reception of Lord Byron's *Cain:*

Literary and Religious Response to Romantic Drama

by

LARRY BRUNNER